EQUIPPING GENERATIONS for Kingdom Advancement

Developing Divine Design for Children and Culture

Book One

Kingdom Curriculum for Families, Schools, and Churches

This is a life-giving core Kingdom curriculum to be integrated with other curriculums.

Published by Doug Carr Freedom Ministry (DCFreedomMinistry)
Printed by Kindle Direct Publishing

ISBN: 978-1-7366952-6-5

Bible Versions Used

Acknowledgements

I am grateful for Adam and Amy Sterenberg from Tree of Life and Path of Life schools. Their encouragement to my wife Pamela and I in our quest to minister to young people increased our hope and made Pam's vision of launching a school for children seem achievable.

I so appreciate Pamela Carr for her continual encouragement, insight, and companionship that makes all of life more possible and enjoyable.

I thank God for Suzanne LeBlanc who continues serving Jesus in so many ways. Suzanne has again edited this book as she has so many others. She sends feedback in a remarkably usable way that helps me complete it with no more than two reviews.

I am grateful for each member of His House Foursquare Church in Sturgis, Michigan who supports our callings, pray for us, and encourage us as we attempt to do great things for God.

I love the input my daughter, Sarah Weekly, provided during the review of the first draft of this book. Sarah answered God's call to teach in public schools and has given her life to help students be the best they can be. I value her thoughts because she has dedicated her career to instructing children at their most formative and sometimes challenging months of Kindergarten.

Table of Contents

Foreword by Adam Sterenberg

Doug and I met over a decade ago. Our church invited him to come and teach on deliverance. The only thing I knew about deliverance was that it was a highly disturbing movie from the 70's. The church scheduled him to come on a Saturday from 9 am – 5 pm. The last place I wanted to be on a Saturday was at church all day. Especially when it was about something I really had no clue about. But I felt a nudge from the Spirit and decided to go. I arrived at church, chose a seat in the back and sat there with my arms crossed. I thought, "if this guy says one flaky thing, I'm outta here."

I stayed the whole day.

Doug was unassuming and down to earth with a dry sense of humor. Although his teaching was extremely foreign to me, it was so Biblical. While at the conference I was delivered of some significant things through corporate prayers—thank you Jesus! Thus began our friendship.

Years prior to our meeting, God called me to start an inner-city Christian school in the Edison Neighborhood called Tree of Life. When I met Doug, our school was a couple of years old. We developed a partnership. Through Tree of Life numerous students, parents, and staff went through **personal deliverance** and inner healing sessions with Dr. Carr. The fruit from his ministry is incredible!

It's with great honor that I write this forward. Doug is one of the most passionate, humble, and well-read Jesus followers that I know. Doug's heart is first and foremost for Jesus and His Kingdom! Doug has done a great job laying out the basic Biblical tenants for Kingdom Advancement. He's broken it down in a way that anyone can use for teaching in a school or educational setting.

Praise God for Dr. Carr!

Preface One: Jesus as a Model

Little is known about Jesus' life as a child, teen, or young man. One Scripture shares a time when Joseph and Mary took Jesus to Jerusalem for Passover. He stayed there, without His parents' knowledge, after they headed home. His parents assumed He was traveling with their extended family. By the end of the day, they began looking for Jesus, but He was not with their group! So, Mary and Joseph headed back to Jerusalem and found Jesus in the temple hanging onto every word of the leaders and asking them questions. People were astonished at his understanding and answers (Luke 2:42–29).

Mary and Joseph were upset and asked why He had not stayed with their family heading home. Jesus answered saying "Did you not know that I must be about My Father's business?" (Luke 2:49)

Three verses later Luke gives a significant glimpse of the Jesus' amazing life and growth as a boy.

📖 And Jesus increased in wisdom and stature, and in favor with God and men. Luke 2:52.

I (Douglas Carr) entered full-time ministry as a Youth for Christ leader in 1973. Luke 2:52 was their key verse from which they drew their "Balanced Life" concept.

Jesus enjoyed a well-rounded balanced upbringing. He grew mentally, physically, spiritually, and socially. Children achieve wholeness when they grow in all these areas. The key to a balanced life is having Jesus in the center of all four of these areas.

To be complete, education must help children grow mentally, physically, spiritually, and socially while keeping Jesus at the center of their lives and activities. Beyond such generalities, however, it is our duty to help children recognize their specific niche and destiny in life.

My contribution to Christian training is helping educators give children a strong spiritual and biblical foundation alongside the rest of their academics. I provide further insight to this in Preface Two.

Preface Two

Equipping Generations
for Kingdom Transformation ~
Vision Overview

There are seven mountains of culture: Family, Religion, Government/Military, Business, Education, Media, and Arts/Entertainment. In 2008, Johnny Enlow shared an eye-opening call for the Ekklesia to impact society with his book, *The Seven Mountain Prophecy: Unveiling the Coming Elijah Revolution*. In 2013, Lance Wallnau and Bill Johnson wrote *Invading Babylon: The 7 Mountain Mandate*. These books encourage parents, teachers, and students to find their best fit to impact society through the Ekklesia and the Kingdom of God.

Note: The Greek Word "Ekklesia" has been translated as "church" since King James permitted the translation of the Bible into the King James Bible. One of King James's conditions is said to be, the word Ekklesia would be replaced with the word "church."

Ekklesia refers to the Legislative Body of Believers called out of this worldly system to reign and rule with Christ. The name "Ekklesia" fell out of favor with King

James, who backed the Bible being published in English. He did place some restrictions, however. He was not comfortable with the idea of any kingdom usurping his authority, so he insisted Ekklesia be translated as "Church." Most Bible translations have followed the King's format since then. I will use the correct word and meaning, "Ekklesia," in this book.

In Matthew 5:13–14, Jesus said Christians are called to be the salt of the earth and the light of the world—*the whole world*—not just in "churches" that meet on Sunday mornings!

While there are numerous variations within each mountain of influence, we have a duty to help children and adults understand God's call to impact all of society with the Gospel: God so loved the WORLD He gave His only begotten son to reform the world to its created order.

We will visit the mountains of culture as children learn to read and write, as well as become proficient in math, science, history, etc. Our aim is to help students establish personal and social values to empower them to be and do everything as God calls them individually.

Our desire is to work with The Holy Spirit, you, and your child. We share our focus from the beginning so together we can help children discover who they are, and the destiny God created for each one.

VISION: Empower generations to transform culture through Kingdom Advancement.

The pivotal verse to our focus comes from the words of Jesus himself:

📖 And from the days of John the Baptist until now the kingdom of heaven suffers violence, and the violent take it by force. Matthew 11:12.

Jesus Christ will not return for a weak, ugly, battered, and defeated bride. He will return for a glorious and victorious bride who has made the enemy a footstool for His feet! Jesus is washing His bride with the water of His Word and restoring His Ekklesia so she will transform the Kingdoms of this World for His rule and reign. He is restoring apostolic order (Ephesians 4:11–16) so every member of the Body may be equipped for the ministry of reconciling the world to God.

The Great Commission commands us to make disciples of ALL NATIONS (Matthew 28:18–20). It is not enough to have "revivals" where Christians are blessed, healed, and empowered, yet remain in selfish isolation from culture, thus limiting their impact on society.

To make disciples of all nations, generations must be equipped to advance the Kingdom of God throughout the seven mountains of culture, which include:

Education, Religion, Family, Business, Government/ Military, Arts/Entertainment, and Media.

MISSION: Thoroughly equip generations to forcefully advance the Kingdom according to God's Prophetic Destiny for each person.

It is the mission of families, churches, and schools to discover and empower each child's gifts, prophetic destiny, and personal desire to serve God according to the tenor of his or her way. Together, they will be the launching pad of Kingdom Exploits to bring Kingdom transformation to every segment of society.

Key Concept: Jesus wants His Kingdom People to reign on earth in every segment of society.

Your kingdom come. Your will be done, On earth as *it is* in heaven. Matthew 6:10.

Now when He was asked by the Pharisees when the kingdom of God would come, He answered them and said, "The kingdom of God does not come with observation; [21] nor will they say, 'See here!' or 'See there!' For indeed, **the kingdom of God is within you.**" Luke 17:20–21.

The following Key Components will be expanded as they cycle through continuing books in this series. Bible characters will be used to illustrate each of these Key Components in the chapters that follow.

KEY COMPONENTS of Christian Education:

1. Students must grow in God's unconditional love, acceptance, and forgiveness. (John)
2. Children must learn they were created on Purpose and for a purpose. (Jeremiah)
3. Children must be guided in their Prophetic Destiny. (Jacob)
4. Children must learn there are no secular pursuits for those who follow God according to His plans and purposes for their lives. (Abraham)
5. Children must mature according to the Tenor of Their Ways.
6. Children must be empowered to align with Gods' Kingdom Government. (Joseph)
7. Children must be equipped to advance the Kingdom of God. (Paul)

Each chapter in this and the following books will revolve around these seven major precepts. Key Bible characters and Scriptures will also be expanded as this series is continued.

We thank you and the Lord for the opportunity to work with you as we minister with you and your child. Never hesitate to call your child's teacher or administration if you have any ideas, questions, or concerns.

~Blessings, Douglas, and Pamela Carr

Introduction

Can you imagine going to a wedding and seeing the bride come down the aisle in dirty old clothes and messy hair? Of course not! The bride does her best to look beautiful when her fiancé walks down the aisle. The groom also looks his best.

The bride and groom's love for each other is the secret ingredient that makes them look so beautiful and handsome. Their exchange of love represents Jesus' love for His Ekklesia and her love for Him. The best beauty treatment Believers have is their reciprocal love with Jesus!

Christians, collectively as the Ekklesia, are called the Bride of Christ. It is important the Ekklesia looks its best as we prepare for the return of Jesus. Jesus wants to equip and empower the Ekklesia to bring reformation to the world before He returns.

The Great Commission states we are to make disciples of ALL NATIONS (Matthew 28:18–20). It is not enough to go to church, have a good time, and feel good about being with God and one another.

To make disciples of all nations, we must learn how to advance the Kingdom in the seven major areas of culture. This will make us look beautiful for God or . . . not! These seven areas are called the "Mountains of Culture." Remember, they include Family, Religion, Government/Military, Business, Education, Media, and Arts/Entertainment.

God has a special plan for each person. He has specific plans for each individual; the special things for Him they were created to do. They may be things big or little, things no one else can do as well as they can. Everyone is specially designed to do special things for God and the world.

God made each one INCREDIBLY special. He loves us so much; He even formed us to *want* to do the very things we can be exceptionally good at. Some people love to draw and color. God gave them that desire. Others like to play with dolls or engage in sports. God placed such desires in the hearts of His children.

I first called this "Kids Curriculum," using "Kids" as an acrostic for "Kids In Divine Service." I now understand, however, this curriculum is for everyone, young and old. Our desire is to help each person realize how much God loves them and His wonderful plan for every individual.

Chapter One

Growing in God's Unconditional Love, Acceptance, and Forgiveness

Key #1: Students must grow in God's unconditional love, acceptance, and forgiveness. (John)

Objective: Students will know Jesus loves them and will become confident and able to give and receive love and openly communicate within safe boundaries.

Benchmark: Students will accept themselves and love themselves and others within a context of accepting one another in a safe environment of respect.

There must be a deliberate tearing down of the strongholds of rejection and abandonment and a pursuit to see the Spirit of Adoption released upon each student.

Key Scriptures:

📖 Now the purpose of the commandment is love from a pure heart, *from* a good conscience, and *from* sincere faith. 1 Timothy 1:5.

📖 And now abide faith, hope, love, these three; but the greatest of these *is* love. 1 Corinthians 13:13.

Today's Focus: Students must be taught God's unconditional love, acceptance, and forgiveness.

Such love is better caught than taught. The life of the teacher is the heart of her/his teaching.

In an atmosphere of love, strongholds of rejection and abandonment can be torn down and replaced with The Spirit of Adoption.

📖 For ye have not received a spirit of bondage again for fear, but ye have received a spirit of adoption, whereby we cry, Abba, Father. Romans 8:15.

Have the students recite (with a preacher's voice, a grownup voice, a quiet or loud voice, etc.) the following verses a few times in various ways today. Be creative with song, puppets, letting different children lead, asking questions about who Timothy was, and what love, having a pure heart, good conscience, and sincere faith is.

📖 Now the purpose of the commandment is love from a pure heart, *from* a good conscience, and *from* sincere faith. 1 Timothy 1:5.

📖 And now abide faith, hope, love, these three; but the greatest of these *is* love. 1 Corinthians 13:13.

Share the following vision in your own words in a way your students will understand. Be attentive to their responses. Expound in creative ways to help each child understand.

VISION: Help each student recognize God's Love for them individually and become channels of God's love to others.

Key Character: The Apostle John, who referred to himself as "the disciple whom Jesus loved."

John was a fisherman when Jesus called him to be a disciple. He didn't fish with fishing poles like we do. He and his companions fished with nets. They worked hard to keep their huge nets in good shape so they could catch lots of fish to sell.

📖 Going on from there, he (Jesus) saw two other brothers, James son of Zebedee and his brother John. They were in a boat with their father Zebedee, preparing their nets. Jesus called them, [22] and immediately they left the boat and their father and followed him. Matthew 4:21–22.

Ask the following questions and guide the conversation to bring understanding:

1. Why do you think James and John were ready to leave their father, their work of fishing, and follow Jesus?

2. Do you think Jesus always call people to leave their jobs to follow him?

Ask if they know people who love, follow, and serve Jesus who work at factories, stores, as police or fire fighters, etc. Mention how many people serve Jesus and others beyond their local church. Their work is done for Jesus as much as a preacher's is. They can serve Jesus and others wherever they work!

Ask if they know anyone who has left previous jobs to serve Jesus in new areas. (Do not limit this to "sacred" employment.) You might use examples of their parents or people they know.

3. Jesus loved John—does that mean that John was perfect? (See what they think and guide the discussion as needed).
4. Ask: "Do you know that John had a bad temper when he first met Jesus?"

📖 James son of Zebedee and his brother John (to them he gave the name Boanerges, which means Sons of Thunder). Mark 3:17.

Ask: "Why do you think John and James were nick-named "Sons of Thunder?" Steer the discussion to include things like: "they were always arguing and fighting," "they had bad tempers, fought with each other, and yelled a lot, etc."

Please do not answer this question out loud. Ask: Do you know anyone who has a bad temper? Would your brother, sister, or parents say you have a bad temper?

Ask: "Does being perfect make God love you, or does receiving God's love make you more like Jesus who is perfect?" (Deal with wrong conceptions of God "loving me because I am good.")

Using some of the Scriptures below, teach how knowing Jesus and walking in love makes us more like Him. Expound on how perfect love drives out fear.

The verses are separated so children can take turns reading them and/or responding to them.

We know that we live in him and he in us, because he has given us of his Spirit. 1 John 4:13.

And we have seen and testify that the Father has sent his Son to be the Savior of the world. 1 John 4:14.

If anyone acknowledges that Jesus is the Son of God, God lives in him and he in God. 1 John 4:15 NIV.

And so we know and rely on the love God has for us. God is love. Whoever lives in love lives in God, and God in him. 1 John 4:16 NIV.

In this way, love is made complete among us so that we will have confidence on the day of

judgment, because in this world we are like him.
1 John 4:17.

📖 There is no fear in love. But perfect love drives out fear, because fear has to do with punishment. The one who fears is not made perfect in love.
1 John 4:19 NIV.

Marvelous things happened to John as he walked with Jesus. He changed so much his nickname was changed from "Son of Thunder" to "Apostle of Love." This wonderful transformation happened as John learned how much Jesus loved him! He became so convinced Jesus loved him, he referred to himself as the "one Jesus loved."

John called himself "The disciple Jesus loved" at least five times in the Gospel of John (John 13:1; 19:26; 20:2; 21:7, and 21:20).

John wrote the Gospel of John and First, Second, and Third John.

1. Why do you think that John felt Jesus loved him so much?
2. How is your life better when you know how much Jesus loves you?
3. What happens when you do not feel loved?

Let them answer and note what their answers reveal about them and their needs.

4. What are some things that make you feel unloved?
5. What are some things that make you feel loved?

Illustrate how Jesus loves them—using their own answers as much as possible.

Ask if any of them do not feel loved? Take note and begin praying against the work of rejection in their lives and pray for the love of Jesus to be released to each one personally.

Prayer time: Wrap up with prayer and a chance to receive and know the love of Jesus. Always be ready to lead children to Jesus. Make sure to record the name and date each child receives Christ. Teachers should arrange (with parent's and pastor's permission) to baptize each child as soon as it works for all involved.

Chapter Two

Created On Purpose and For a Purpose

Key #2: Children must learn they were created on Purpose and for a purpose. (Jeremiah)

Objective: Students will recognize and accept themselves as God's special creation with a unique creative purpose assigned specifically for each one.

Benchmark: Each student will recognize God's special purpose and design for their lives. They will sense God's personal call on their life. Hence, they will mature according to their God-given bent until they are better established and able to test and know God's specific design for their lives.

Key Scripture:

📖 For I know the thoughts that I think toward you, says the Lord, thoughts of peace and not of evil, to give you a future and a hope. Jeremiah 29:11.

📖 For I know the plans I have for you," declares the Lord, "plans to prosper you and not to harm you, plans to give you hope and a future.
Jeremiah 29:11 NIV.

Suggested songs: "He's still working on me." "I am a Promise." (You may use one of these links for I am a Promise.) The first shares the lyrics to help them learn them. The second can be used for performance.

https://youtu.be/mIQJcusRt9E with lyrics.

https://youtu.be/O62lOLUjW90 no lyrics

Key Character: Jeremiah.

Focus: Children must learn they were created on purpose and for a purpose.

Suggested puppet skit or role play. Find a way to demonstrate how people are happier when they become who God created them to be.

Can anyone quote Ephesians 2:10?

📖 For we are His workmanship, created in Christ Jesus for good works, which God prepared beforehand that we should walk in them. Ephesians 2:10.

We have looked at how much God loves us and how ready He is to accept us and forgive us. We need to know we belong to God to develop a heart to serve God.

Ask some of the following questions:

➢ How many different colors of hair do you see in this room?

➢ How many boys are here? How many girls are here?

➢ Do any of you feel like you are too big for your age?

➢ How many of you feel like you are too small for your age?

It is amazing. God made each person so special, even twins are not exactly alike!

Point out some ways God made each person special and not like anyone else.

God doesn't make any mistakes—ever! He did not make a mistake when He created each of you exactly the way He did.

Some people have birth marks and others do not. All are special. Some have handicaps and others do not. They are all special in God's sight. It is important to accept how God made us and be thankful we are special to Him.

God created each one of us as He did. No one is a mistake. Even when children do not know their birth mother or birth father, they were created on purpose and for a purpose.

God says, "He is a father to the father-less." There are at least 31 Bible verses saying God has a special relationship with children who do not know their birth parents.

The two most familiar are in Psalm 68:5–6.

📖 A father of the fatherless, a defender of widows, Is God in His holy habitation. ⁶ God sets the solitary in families. He brings out those who are bound into prosperity; But the rebellious dwell in a dry land. Psalm 68:5–6.

📖 Pure and undefiled religion before God and the Father is this: to visit orphans and widows in their trouble, *and* to keep oneself unspotted from the world. James 1:27.

Children who do not know their birth father or mother, or those who have parents with lots of problems, were created special by God too. He has great plans for every life, regardless of how it begins. Jesus rose above His circumstances. He was conceived by the Holy Spirit, and even though Joseph took Mary to be his wife after the angel spoke to him, they never lived as man and wife until after Jesus was born in a stable. Jesus was a special child begotten of God, but people accused Jesus of being the illegitimate child of Joseph and Mary.

God pays extra attention to children who do not live with their birth mother and/or father. He will use their hard circumstances and trials to make them stronger as overcomers. He will also use them to help others who may not feel loved or accepted. We all have different beginnings and diverse lives, but God is maker of us all.

Have the children recite a few of the following verses in various ways today. Be creative with song, puppets, letting different children lead, asking questions about who Jeremiah was and how God made him on purpose for a purpose.

Can anyone explain who Jeremiah was and how God made him on purpose for a special purpose?

Let's look at some verses from Jeremiah Chapter 1.

📖 Then the word of the Lord came to me, saying: [5] "Before I formed you in the womb I knew you; Before you were born I sanctified you; I ordained you a prophet to the nations." Jeremiah 1:4–5.

How do you think Jeremiah felt when the Lord spoke Jeremiah 1:4–5 to him? Give them time to discuss this.

What are some excuses you might come up with if God said you are going to be a prophet and speak to nations? Have someone read the excuse Jeremiah gave in verse six.

📖 Then said I: "Ah, Lord God! Behold, I cannot speak, for I *am* a youth." Jeremiah 1:6.

Look at how God responded to Jeremiah's thinking he was not ready to serve God.

📖 But the Lord said to me: "Do not say, 'I *am* a youth,' For you shall go to all to whom I send you, And whatever I command you, you shall speak. [8] Do not be afraid of their faces, For I *am* with you to deliver you," says the Lord. Jeremiah 1:7-8.

God's calling is God's enabling!

God often calls people to do things that seem impossible for them. But when people say "YES" to God, He makes everything possible, for nothing is impossible for God. God wants to do for you what He did for Jerimiah. Look!

First, God touched Jeremiah. That is anointing!

📖 Then the Lord put forth His hand and touched my mouth, and the Lord said to me:
Jeremiah 1:9a.

Then God equipped Jeremiah!

📖 "Behold, I have put My words in your mouth [10] See, I have this day set you over the nations and over the kingdoms.
Jeremiah 1:9b–10a.

Next, God assigned Jeremiah!

📖 To root out and to pull down, to destroy and to throw down, To build and to plant."
Jeremiah 1:10b.

Key Character: Jeremiah.

Ask: How do you think Jeremiah felt when he found out God had a purpose for him even before he was born?

Ask: If God speaks to you about your purpose, will you be afraid or excited?

God not only knew Jeremiah, but He also knew what Jeremiah was created to be and to do in life.

Likewise, God gave each one of you a plan and purpose even before you were born! (Refer back to Jeremiah 29:11 and have one of the children explain it.)

God did not create Jeremiah to sit in a corner playing video games or watching T.V. He created him to BE someone special and DO special things for God.

What do you think is most important in God's eyes: BEING or DOING? (Let them explain and share their ideas. Take notes because you might pick up on some wrong thinking that God will use you to correct).

God created us to be human BEINGS not human DOINGS. He is far more interested in who we are than

He is in what we do. He is more concerned we BE Christians than He is having us DO good things. He also knows that if we walk with Him and become what he created us to BE, we will DO what he created us to do.

The Bible teaches what we DO flows from who we ARE.

📖 A good man out of the good treasure of his heart brings forth good; and an evil man out of the evil treasure of his heart brings forth evil. For out of the abundance of the heart his mouth speaks. Luke 6:45.

Think about what this verse tells us. If good things come from your mouth—what does that say about your heart? (Give them time to answer.)

And if bad things come from your mouth—what does that say about your heart? (Have them give examples of some of the good things that come from the mouths of children with good hearts.)

Ask: "Can you say the right words with the wrong heart?" Press into this until they understand if they say "I love you" with a snotty attitude or "I'm sorry" with anger or pride such wrong stuff is still flowing from a wrong heart.

Ask: "If our words show us that something is wrong with our heart—what can we do about it?" Again, take time to listen. Part of our duty is to reinforce correct thinking and bring them into right thinking according to what the Bible says.

What do you think would happen if a cat tried to bark or a dog tried to meow? It wouldn't be right because God created cats to be cats and do cat stuff. God created dogs to be dogs and do dog stuff. Cows cannot fly and birds cannot give milk, because God created cows to give milk and birds to fly.

You can be what God wants you to be. As you become what God created you to BE, you will do what God Almighty created you to DO.

Read Jeremiah 29:11 again and ask the students "Is following God's plans to prosper you as sure as a dog barking because God created him to bark?"

(Lead their discussion to the conclusion that people must CHOOSE to follow God in order to know the plans that HE has to prosper them, give them a hope and a future).

Teach them sin is choosing NOT to follow God or to enter the plans that God has for each one. You may want to lead them in asking forgiveness in areas where they know they have not followed God's plans. Then lead them in a commitment to follow God and to seek the plans that HE has for them.

Note for leaders: In Christ we can be partakers of His divine nature. This begins at salvation and is developed through prayer, guidance, and loving discipleship. This begins at salvation and increases as people learn to trust and obey Jesus.

Until people are born again, they have carnal soulish natures which can never please God. A new nature is formed in them when they are born again.

📖 Therefore, if anyone *is* in Christ, *he is* a new creation; old things have passed away; behold, all things have become new. 2 Corinthians 5:17

The new creation is both instant and gradual. Jesus takes up residence in a Believer's spirit immediately when they are saved. From there, they can choose to be partakers of the divine nature. Most people need help to understand and choose to walk it.

📖 Grace and peace be multiplied to you in the knowledge of God and of Jesus our Lord, ³ as His divine power has given to us all things that *pertain* to life and godliness, through the knowledge of Him who called us by glory and virtue, ⁴ by which have been given to us exceedingly great and precious promises, that through these you may be **partakers of the divine nature**, having escaped the corruption *that is* in the world through lust. 2 Peter 1:2-4.

Chapter Three

Guiding Children in Their Prophetic Destiny

Key #3: Children must be guided in their Prophetic Destiny. (Jacob/Israel)

Jacob, whose name was changed to Israel, will illustrate coming into God's prophetic destiny.

Objective: Students will be guided and helped to discern their prophetic destiny and how God wants them to prepare for what He has for them in life. (Following their personal interests will help them discover God's call on their lives.)

Benchmark: Students will have a God-ordained sense of His destiny and call on their lives. They will have a developing response to the question: "What do you think God wants you to do when you grow up?"

Focus: Children must learn their prophetic destiny and be exposed to it and guided to learn about it. As they grow, they should be offered opportunities to investigate various career paths they are interested in.

Parents and teachers must prayerfully seek to help each child discover their destiny and expose him or her to it.

Our key verse for this lesson speaks about the prophetic destiny God has for each person.

Key Scripture:

📖 For we are His workmanship, created in Christ Jesus for good works, which God prepared beforehand that we should walk in them. Ephesians 2:10.

Wherever God calls you to serve will be the most spiritual place you can serve! God loves you so much, He puts a desire in your heart to do things you really like to do to bless God and people.

(Giving opportunities for those who are drawn to sing solos, help with puppets, clean the classroom, read stories, or Bible verses, etc. will help reveal prophetic destiny.)

"Prophetic" means God spoke what He knows is best for you to be and do before you were even born. God has prepared good works in advance for each one you.

"Destiny" means God's absolute best plan and design for each of you. God has a perfect plan for your life.

Jesus came so you might have life more abundantly as you walk according to His plans for each of your lives.

The devil wants to steal, kill, and destroy God's perfect plans for each life, so it is important to say yes to Jesus and no to the devil (John 10:10).

Ephesians 2:10 says you are God's workmanship. Ask, "Do you think God makes any junk or mistakes?" (Be on guard for any wrong thinking and follow the Holy Spirit in addressing it.)

The New Testament was written in Greek and the word translated "workmanship" is pronounced *"poy'-ay-mah."* The English word "poem" comes from this word. God wants to make a beautiful poem or story of your life!

(Note for leaders: this is Strongs Number: G4161 and comes from the root word, which comes from Strongs Number 4160 and means "a product, i.e., fabric (literally or figuratively). It refers to something that is thing made, workmanship, particularly, the work of God the creator.)

God has good plans for each life.

📖 For I know the thoughts that I think toward you, says the Lord, thoughts of peace and not of evil, to give you a future and a hope. Jeremiah 29:11.

📖 For I know the plans I have for you," declares the Lord, "plans to prosper you and not to harm you, plans to give you hope and a future. Jeremiah 29:11 NIV.

(You can reinforce verses in different ways. You may instruction the children to say them LOUD and then say them QUIET, LOUD, SERIOUS, or like a little kid or old man, etc.)

Suggested songs: Jesus loves me, this I know. This Little Light of Mine, or I will make you fishers of men.

Ask, "Where do you go to catch fish?" Then ask, "Where do you go to catch people for Jesus. You must go to wherever they are. God needs fishers of men who go to school, work in stores, run businesses, and serve hamburgers at McDonalds.

Help them understand God may call them to serve Jesus as a public-school teacher, businessperson, or whatever. Wherever God calls you to serve will be the most spiritual place you can serve!

(Paying attention to what they like to do helps leaders discern their prophetic destinies.)

Help them understand God may call them to serve Him as a teacher, businessperson, policeman, fireman, garbage collector, or whatever for their good and His glory.

Have them name some jobs they might like to do. Inquire why they picked the ones they mentioned.

Encourage them; wherever God calls each of you to serve will be the happiest and most spiritual place you can serve! (You may begin to look for those who are drawn to sing solos, help with puppets, clean the classroom, read stories, or Bible verses, etc.)

Here's a suggested topic for a puppet skit, role play, or clowning, etc. It would be great to have a puppet feel bad because he is doing something great in the "world" but nothing much in the "church." You can then have another puppet or two help the first one see that he IS serving God—right where God wants him to serve. (Puppets, clowns, or role play can be used as hyperbole to really get the point across.)

Pointer for Ministers to Children: I urge you to have a prayer list for the children and to pray for each child by name at least once a week. Your prayer list should include a listening time where you ask God for revelation as to which of the Seven Mountains of Culture Jesus wants to use them in: Family, Government/Military, Business, Education, Religion, Media, or Arts and Entertainment.

You might consider inviting people from different occupations to share with the students what they do for a living. (Examples: people who serve in business, government, counseling, education, etc.)

Many children will be called to be molders of Kingdom values within one or another of these mountains of culture.

Focus: Children need encouragement to advance the Kingdom at some level of society. God wants to use this generation to forcibly advance the Kingdom of God and bring true transformation to society. Help them see their part as God answers the prayer "thy kingdom come; thy will be done on EARTH as it is in Heaven.

📖 From the days of John the Baptist until now, the kingdom of heaven has been forcefully advancing, and forceful men lay hold of it. Matthew 11:12.

Reinforce this verse in different ways today. Make sure they understand the connection between the Kingdom of heaven and the kingdoms of this world.

Optional: Review Key Scriptures from Appendix A.

Can anyone quote the verses we've already learned?

It might be good to have small prizes for those who can and develop a system of recording who can say their verses. We will probably repeat the memory verses once every seven weeks during the first year or so. You also may want them to quote their verses before their class or congregation when they know them well enough.

The following are ideas for stories, puppet skits, role play, or clowning:

- Recruit someone gifted with puppets to lead the children in a skit or role play of Kingdom people influencing society. If you have students with clown, puppet, or acting skills, encourage them to act out this subject.
- A skit about how a naughty boy or girl can be transformed by the power of God's love which is manifested through someone who genuinely loves God would be good.
- A story about George Washington Carver or William Wilberforce would also be excellent here. (You can research them online or in a library.)
- It would be great to have a puppet feel bad because he is doing something great in the "world" but nothing much in the "church" You can then have another puppet or two help the first one see that he IS serving God—right where God wants him to serve. (Puppets, clowns, or role play can be used as hyperbole to really get the point across).

Key Character: Jacob/Israel

I want you to meet an interesting character today. He was given the name Jacob but when he was older, God changed his name to Israel.

God had great plans for Jacob before he was ever born. So did the devil! God created Jacob to advance God's kingdom on earth—but the devil wanted him to be a liar!

Jesus said the thief (the devil) wants to kill, steal, and destroy. Not good! God wants people to enjoy life that is abundant and full. Jacob had good times and bad times, but as he learned to trust God, he was brought into God's prophetic destiny for his life.

Jacob's father, Isaac, prayed for his wife Rebekah to get pregnant before Jacob was conceived. He got more than he asked for! Rebekah became pregnant with two sons! Let's read the beginning of his story. (Take volunteers who can read well—it is great when they have their own Bibles.) I suggest the NKJV because it flows well and is more accurate than many translations. We will begin with Genesis 25:21-26.

📖 Now Isaac pleaded with the Lord for his wife, because she *was* barren; and the Lord granted his plea, and Rebekah his wife conceived. 22 But the children struggled together within her; and she said, "If *all is* well, why *am I like* this?" So she went to inquire of the Lord. 23 And the Lord said to her:

📖 "Two nations *are* in your womb, Two peoples shall be separated from your body; *One* people shall be stronger than the other, And the older shall serve the younger."

📖 24 So when her days were fulfilled *for her* to give birth, indeed *there were* twins in her womb. 25 And the first came out red. *He was* like a hairy garment all over; so they called his name Esau. 26 Afterward his brother came out, and his hand took hold of Esau's heel; so his name was called Jacob. Isaac *was* sixty years old when she bore them.

The name "Jacob" means "deceiver or liar." How do you think Jacob felt about his name?

People may believe negative names they are called, rather than what God says about them.

Sometimes smart kids are called stupid and end up believing they are stupid, so they fail to be as intelligent as God made them to be.

Good looking children may be called ugly, and if they believe such insults, it will steal their beauty. Their smiles may turn to frowns and the light in their eyes may dim.

To become everything God wants you to be, it is important for you to start believing what God thinks about you, not what people who pick on you call you.

This may be a good time to lead students in forgiving people who have called them names. Once they have done so, you can help them renounce negative names they have been called and speak the opposite in their lives.

Pointer for Leaders: I have people make a bowl out of their hands and then place in the bowl what people did to hurt them and how it made them feel.

Once they have filled their bowl, I encourage them to forgive people who hurt them and ask God to break the power of hurtful words.

As I mentioned earlier, later in Jacob's life, his name was changed to Israel. God had great plans for Jacob before he was ever born—so did the devil.

God has a perfect plan for every person's life—even if they have trouble getting along with their brothers or sisters!

Jacob and Esau were so different it was hard to believe they were from the same family. Ask: "have you ever felt like you did not belong to your family? Why?" Reassure them God had great plans for Jacob and Esau even though there were times they did not get along very well.

Jacob became a "momma's boy" as he grew. He liked hanging around his mom in the house and in the kitchen. His mother, Rebekah, favored Jacob.

Esau was a "daddy's boy" as he grew up. Esau loved being outdoors. He became a great deer hunter. His father, Isaac, favored him and loved eating venison.

These two brothers did not like each other and played their parents against each other. We will look at that another time.

Does anybody feel like your mom or dad loves your brother or sister more than you? (Let them share why they feel that way.)

Does anyone feel like your mom or dad loves you most? (Again, let them share why they feel that way.) Take notes so you will know what to target in prayer.

Part of our ministry is helping each child recognize he or she is special to God and that God has something special for them to do.

Some other time we will see how Jacob had twelve sons who become the heads of the twelve tribes of Israel.

Chapter Four

No Secular Pursuits for Those Who Follow God

Key #4: Children must learn there are no secular pursuits for those who follow God according to His plans and purposes for their lives. Abraham life shows how this works.

Children must learn they were created on purpose, both to BE and Do according as God destines them.

Objective: The students will learn they can do whatever they do for the glory of God (1 Corinthians 10:31). Destroy the False dualism of sacred and secular and help students realize doing whatever God leads them to is sacred in His eyes.

Benchmark: Students will be able to state the general field of the occupation they are drawn to and how God will use them in it. They will understand whatever God calls them to do, becomes sacred as they prepare to follow God in whatever field He leads them to.

Jesus said, "I will make you fishers of men." Ask if anyone likes to fish. Ask them if they fish in their backyard and why or why not. Try to emphasize that to fish you must go where the fish are, and to win people for Jesus you must go where people without Jesus are.

Pointer for Teachers: The spirit of religion has somehow convinced Believers to think what they do in church is sacred and what they do outside of church is secular. This false dualism between sacred and secular has caused people to think that teaching Sunday School in church is sacred and teaching in a public school is secular. Such thinking has taken the salt out of the earth and the light out of the world. Therefore, the seven mountains of culture do not have the presence and influence of Believers they need.

The Seven Mountains of Education, Religion, Family, Business, Government/Military, Arts/Entertainment, and Media tend to separate God from the so called "secular" pursuits. We must train children to take God's salt and light into the entire world and into all professions so they can advance the Kingdom of God in all areas of culture.

Focus: Children must learn there are no secular pursuits for those who follow God according to His plans and purposes for their lives. They must learn whatever God calls them to do is sacred whether being a teacher, a businessman, or a preacher.

Key Scripture:

📖 Whatever you do, work at it with all your heart, as working for the Lord, not for human masters, 24 since you know that you will receive an inheritance from the Lord as a reward. It is the Lord Christ you are serving.
Colossians 3:23–24. NIV.

Reinforce this verse in different ways today. You may ask them if a person can be a carpenter for God — or be a Walmart clerk or a street cleaner for God. You may want to work on this passage one phrase at a time to make sure they get it.

Remind them of Jeremiah 29:11 to help them know God has wonderful thoughts and plans in mind for each one of them.

📖 For I know the thoughts that I think toward you, says the Lord, thoughts of peace and not of evil, to give you a future and a hope. Jeremiah 29:11.

📖 For I know the plans I have for you," declares the Lord, "plans to prosper you and not to harm you, plans to give you hope and a future.
Jeremiah 29:11. NIV

Review other Scriptures as led from Appendix A.

Suggested songs: "I will make you fishers of men." Try to emphasize to fish you must go to where the fish are, and to win lost people for Jesus you must go to where people who do not know Jesus personally are.

Idea for puppet skit or role play or clowning. Plan something about taking risks for God. You may tell the story of Jim Elliot and his widow who returned to the tribe that murdered her husband. (Google it or ask an older student to Google and give a report on it.)

Key Character: Abraham. Can anyone tell me who the Bible calls "The Father of our faith?" Lead the discussion until someone comes up with Abraham.

Romans 4:11–12 says Abraham is the Father of Faith to all who believe in Jesus.

> And he received the sign of circumcision, a seal of the righteousness of the faith which *he had while still* uncircumcised, that he might be the father of all those who believe, though they are uncircumcised, that righteousness might be imputed to them also, ¹² and the father of circumcision to those who not only *are* of the circumcision, but who also walk in the steps of the faith which our father Abraham *had while still* uncircumcised. Romans 4:11–12

Ask: What do you think the Father of Faith might do for a job? Encourage them to share.

This is not the time to correct wrong answers. Let them share whatever they think at this point. Listen to their ideas and jot down their key points.

After they share for a bit, say: Abraham the Father of Faith never preached a sermon or taught a Sunday School lesson. He was not a pastor, nor an elder in his church, or a deacon. He never sang on a worship team. Does this surprise you?

So why is Abraham called the Father of Faith? **It is because he moved by faith into the work and into the places where God told him to go. He left the familiar to move to places God would show him . . . he moved before he knew everything about where he was going.**

The Lord had said to Abram, "Go from your country, your people and your father's household to the land I will show you. ² "I will make you into a great nation, and I will bless you; I will make your name great, and you will be a blessing. ³ I will bless those who bless you, and whoever curses you I will curse; and all peoples on earth will be blessed through you." Genesis 12:1–3.

Abraham was named "Abram" by his parents. God later changed his name to Abraham. We will study his name change another time.

Today it is important to help your students understand how God sent Abraham to be a missionary in a foreign land, even though he was not a preacher, a trained missionary, or a medical doctor.

God sent Abraham as a husband, a shepherd and as a father to be into a dark land that was without God.

Abraham was called to leave his home, his hometown, and his family to go to the land God would show him. Now, when people go on long trips, they use Global Positioning System (GPS) or directions from Map Quest. They have everything planned before they begin their journey. Not Abram! All God told him was, "leave here and go to the place *I will show you.*"

Abraham had to step out by faith—chasing a whole new idea from God. He was like a businessman starting a new business with just an idea like Colonel Harland Sanders who started Kentucky Fried Chicken (KFC) in 1929.

Have you ever eaten KFC? Colonel Harland Sanders started Kentucky Fried Chicken in 1929. He was born to a Christian family, but his father died when he was 5 years old. His mother had to work, so Harland had to cook for his family. His mom later married a man who beat Harland so much, he quit school and ran away from home in 7th grade. He worked a lot of jobs: steamboat pilot, insurance salesman, railroad fireman, a farmer, and joined the army when he was 16 by lying about his age. (We do not recommend lying!)

After coming home from Cuba, where he served in the Army, a lot of things started going wrong for Colonel Sanders. He nearly went bankrupt, his first wife left him. He missed his daughter so much he was tempted to kidnap her and run away. But God wasn't finished with Colonel Sanders yet and He helped the Colonel overcome the temptation to do the wrong thing.

God gave Colonel Sanders the idea of cooking chicken for customers who came to his gas station. People liked his food, and more and more people came to his "food mart" gas station where he served chicken. Later, the Freeway I-75 was built and took most of the business away from Colonel Sander's gas station. It looked like his business would not make it. But God had a better idea! The Lord gave him a new idea and he began selling Kentucky Fried Chicken Franchises and they made $520.3 million dollars in 2007. Wow—what an idea!

God gave Abram an idea— "go to the land that I will show you." Abram knew God's voice, but he did not know any of the details. This required great faith. Abram followed God and did what God led him to do. He became a businessman who moved several times as the Lord led him. It took Abram's faith and obedience to make him the Father of the Faith.

God told Abraham all the nations of earth would be blessed through him. This prophecy was fulfilled thousands of years later when Jesus was born of the Virgin Mary.

God has special ideas for every person. These ideas are His prophetic destiny for every boy, girl, and man and woman.

Ideas flow according to the tenor of one's way. God ideas help people do the good works that God created in advance for them to do.

Occasionally, God gives the whole idea at once, but usually He only gives one step at a time. Abraham had to take one step each time God told him to do something new.

This requires faith and obedience; God blesses and leads people to fulfill the whole idea that God has for their lives. I want to pray today that God will give you at least the start of the idea that He has for each of you.

Chapter Five

Maturing Children According to the Tenor of Their Ways

Key #5: Children must mature according to the Tenor of Their Ways.

Objective: Guide students to discover, accept, and embrace the tenor of their ways.

Benchmark: Students will be able to share and explain how God has uniquely created them and gave them specific desires to do God's will in God's way. They will be able to define the tenor of his/her way.

Key Scripture:

📖 Train up the child according to the tenor of his way, and when he is old he will not depart from it. Proverbs 22:6 DARBY

This training can be enhanced by exposure to people with similar tenors and possibly doing internships with them.

Pointer for Teachers: Satan hates the God-given uniqueness of every child. He is bent on making children ashamed of the very things God gave them to make them special. He will use the iniquities of the ancestors to divert children from God's best.

The devil uses sibling rivalry to impede progress in discovering one's personal gifting, calling, and tenor of their way. Sadly, the devil often uses hurtful things people say (or the way they say them) to make children feel worthless, hopeless, stupid, etc.

Name calling, ridicule, peer pressure, teasing, and lies of the devil, etc. stifle one's acceptance of their tenor. This leads many to having faulty identities and/or self-concepts. It is important for parents and educators to discover and reinforce God's given tenor for each student.

It is vital we help students recognize and develop within the tenor of their individual God-given design and nature.

The tenor of one's way is linked to their destiny!

Tenor refers to the God-given bent in each child. Some children were created to be quiet, others loud. Some are athletic, others are studious or musical. Some children enjoy being inside, others want to be outdoors. Some like crowds, others would rather be alone or with just a few people. It is important to discover the tenor placed in each child by God.

The word tenor comes from Middle English; from Old French tenour, from Latin tenor course, substance, import of a law', from tenere 'to hold."

Surprisingly, tenor comes from the Hebrew word "darak" which means to tread or march and refers to the road or way one should march. It is used in Numbers 24:17 and translated "shall come" as in "A star *shall come* forth from Jacob."

Tenor refers to the specific road or way God creates for each child to walk. It would be shameful to force one whose tenor is being a preacher, to be an athlete or vice-versa. If God created a child to be athletic, the child should be exposed to athletic activities. If they are designed to be musical, then music lessons will help the child become whom God created them to be.

Focus: It is important each child learns and embraces his or her God-given unique and personal tenor of his or her way. Ideally, parents and teachers discover what God has already placed within each child so they can help develop it.

It is shameful to go against God's tenor for children or adults. It is a mistake when parents force their personal bents and desires on their child.

It harms children when parents who were successful (or unsuccessful) in a particular area try molding children in the image of the parent(s) dreams rather than the dreams God gives them.

If God places a specific tenor in a child, music for example, it would be going against God to force the child to conform to a parent's desire of having a star athlete. Children must learn to follow their God-given flow even when their peers are more interested in other things.

God knew each child before He formed them in the womb. For example, He set Jeremiah apart with a tenor to be a prophet, and David with a tenor to be a songwriter and king.

This is more than prophetic destiny. It is prophetic destiny linked to the tenor of each child's way.

This is clearly seen in the prophetic word God gave Abraham about Isaac.

📖 Then God said: "No, Sarah your wife shall bear you a son, and you shall call his name Isaac; I will establish My covenant with him for an everlasting covenant, *and* with his descendants after him. Genesis 17:19.

God created Isaac to be a covenant keeper and a father of promise.

Ask students to share their ideas of what family is. There are lots of ideas on family, some are excellent because they follow God's plan for the immediate family to be a mother and father who love each other within the covenant of marriage.

Reinforce tenor in various ways. You might sing the children's song "I am a Promise." There are several great versions of it on the computer children can sing with. This is a great song for children and parents. A couple of my favorites are found in these links, which were shared in a previous lesson.

https://youtu.be/mIQJcusRt9E with lyrics.

https://youtu.be/O62lOLUjW90 no lyrics

Ask the children what they most like to do. What they share helps reveal the tenor of each student's way. Encourage each child with statements like: Aren't you glad God gave you special things you like to do?

Ask "How many of you like ice cream?" Then ask "which is your favorite kind (flavor) of ice cream? The things you really like or do not like to eat is part of the tenor or your ways.

God created the rainbow as a promise the world would never again be destroyed by a flood like happened in Noah's day. God uses rainbows in the sky to remind us of His promises.

Rainbows are pretty because they have more than one color. Their contrasting colors makes them special.

God's "rainbow" promise over each of you is different, which makes every one of you extra special.

Ask again: what are some of your favorite things to do? If more than one child answers, you can point out each child's answer is right for them—it is the tenor of their ways. Teachers are responsible to seek each child's tenor out and help them develop within. Children seldom become bored and listless when they are developing according to their induvial bents.

As led, review Scriptures from Appendix A.

Here's an idea for puppet skit or role play or clowning. Plan something around a person who feels like they should be a hairdresser . . . but struggles because others think they should be a pastor. Demonstrate how the person has a much more effective "field of harvest" by working in a beauty shop where he/she can listen to problems people have and then tell them how God can help?

Parents have children who become sons and daughters who will grow and become mothers and fathers. God's idea of family, however, carries on from generation to generation. Moms and Dads have children who grow up and get married and have more children. The Bible has many records of such families. It calls them "genealogies."

Genealogies give family trees and tell the story of families. There are short genealogies like the one in Genesis 4:1–2 that talks about Adam and Eve and their first two sons. It says one raised sheep and the other planted crops.

A longer genealogy in Genesis lists each family by the heads of families from Adam to Noah (Genesis 5:1–32).

Ask the children to share what they know about their grandparents. See how many generations they are aware of. If adults are present, you might ask them the same question.

God is so concerned about children, parents, grandparents, great grandparents, great-great grandparents, etc. He shares forty-two generations in the Gospel of Matthew and more than that in Luke! That is like repeating "great" forty-two times to get to your forty-second grandparents.

Matthew and Luke both have long genealogies (Matthew 1:1–17 and Luke 3:23–38). They give the family tree of Jesus. The family tree in Matthew starts with Abraham and mentions fourteen generations from Abraham to David, fourteen from David to the exile, and fourteen more from the exile to Jesus. Luke gives the same lineage but goes all the way back to Adam!

Tell the students, God knows what parents, great grandparents, great-great grandparents do can affect children for good or bad.

Ask students to share really great things some of their parents, grandparents and further back have done. You may also carefully ask if anyone in their family line has done anything bad. Do not shame students but encourage them because God can take children of bad family lines and make them extra special.

Good news! God loves and uses people even if they and/or their mom or dad have really messed up. Remember Abram and Isaac told their wives to lie and say they were sisters rather than wives.

God still used them in great ways after they quit lying. Revelation 21:8 includes liars in a list of people who will not go to heaven unless they change. But God used Abraham and Isaac even after they lied and called their wives "sisters."

They were both afraid they might be killed by people whose cities they were passing through so strangers could marry their wives.

Three stories in Genesis tell how Abram (Abraham) or Isaac told their wives to claim they were their sisters and pretend they were not married.

The first one is in Genesis 12:10–20. Abraham later moved to ancient Egypt his country was running out of food.

Abram and his wife who was also his half-sister, Sarai pronounced "Sari" (later called Sarah) moved to where people did not love God or obey the Bible. Sarai was strikingly beautiful. Abram was fearful and asks her to say she is only his sister so the Egyptians would not kill him so they could take her.

Pharoah and the Egyptians saw how beautiful Sarai was. The Egyptian princes showered Abram with gifts of livestock and servants to gain her hand in marriage. Sarai thus becomes part of "Pharaoh's house." God was not happy about it and sent a plague., making it impossible for their women to have babies. Pharaoh restored Sarai to Abram and ordered them to leave Egypt. (Even ungodly people know lying is bad.)

Later, in Genesis 20:1–6 Abraham traveled to the southern region of Gerar. There, King Abimelech noticed how beautiful Sarah was. Abraham told him Sarah was his sister. (She was his wife!)

God intervened before Abimelech even touched Sarah. Abimelech complained to Abraham. Abraham tried to excuse his lie by saying Sarah really is his half-sister, even though they were married.

Abimelech restored Sarah to Abraham and gave him gifts of livestock and servants by way of apology. He allowed Abraham to reside anywhere in Gerar. Abimelech also gave 1,000 pieces of silver to Abraham. Abraham prayed for King Abimelech and his subjects, so their wives could conceive children again.

Unfortunately, Isaac did not learn from his father's mistakes. Iniquities are troubling bents or distortions of character that can pass from parents and grandparents to children.

The Bible says the iniquities of parents and grandparents can be passed down three or four generations to the children. Iniquities are patterns of bad behaviors passed down family lines. For example, the children of mad dads may become angry boys and girls. Children of alcoholics tend to become alcoholics later in life. Thankfully, that can be prevented, and we will talk about that later.

In Genesis 26:1–33, Isaac moves to the southern part of Gerar to avoid another food shortage.

God told Isaac to move there and told him not to go through Egypt. God promised to fulfill the oath He made to Abraham through Isaac.

Isaac turned to lying just like his father had. That is how patterns of iniquity work if they are not broken. Isaac said his wife Rebekah was really his sister because he was afraid the Philistines might kill him to marry Rebekah. A while later, the King saw Isaac smooching Rebekah and accused Isaac of lying. He confronted him. Isaac admitted his lying and he and the King became friends.

Thank God, we do not need to repeat the iniquities of our parents and grandparents. So, what can we do about the bad things we inherit from parents and grandparents?

Jesus shed His blood so we can be forgiven and set free from our own sins and the iniquities (bent, twisting, or distortion of character) passed down from our Fathers.

Isaiah 53:5 says Jesus was bruised for our iniquities. He bled underneath his skin for the iniquities we have inherited from our parents, their parents, and so on.

Isaac inherited his lying and putting his wife in bad situations from his father. Ask the children if they have inherited anything bad from their parents or grandparents. Do not ask them to publicly share them but ask them to raise their hands if they see naughty things moods or behaviors God will not bless in their lives that are similar to things they see in their families. (Some examples are lying, getting mad, being moody, not respecting others, eating too much, or resisting what God or others tells them to do.)

Pray a generic prayer over them. A sample prayer is:

Jesus, the Bible tells us we can inherit good things and bad things from our parents and grandparents. You shed your blood for the bad attitudes and behaviors we have like our parents and grandparents have. Today we confess we have these iniquities (you might have them whisper them to God). Give them a moment and then continue in prayer.

Jesus, we apply the blood from Your bruises and ask you to forgive and cleanse us from these iniquities. (Have them again whisper them to God.)

Jesus, we thank You for cleansing us. We ask you to make us more like You and Your Father in heaven. Amen.

Notes for leaders:

Curses. The Bible says curses can flow down family lines for several generations and blessings can flow down for a thousand generations. Children may have curses that must be broken from family lines.

Family blessings can be restored even without knowledge of family lines by asking God to release blessings from a thousand generations and to break every curse from four to ten generations. Curses often need breaking off family lines before blessings can be applied to children. The Holy Spirit desires for every curse and iniquity to be broken off students. He will guide teachers in doing this through prayer. The children can receive through such prayers.

Iniquities. A search can be made for "iniquity" and "iniquities" in the King James or New King James bible in Bible Gateway.

Only eight of sixty-four Bibles I've studied, correctly translate the Hebrew word "Avon" as iniquity. The others wrongly substitute "sin or sins." Sins are things people do or do not do according to God's will. Iniquities are patterns of perversity passed down through bloodlines. *Breaking Patterns of Perversity ~ Freedom from Iniquity* and *From Woe is Me to Wow is He!* by Douglas E Carr are great recourses for parents, teachers, and intercessors who want to free children to come into God's tenor of their ways.

Chapter Six

Empowering Children to Align With Gods' Kingdom Government

Key #6: Children must be empowered to align with Gods' Kingdom Government. (Joseph)

Objective: Students will understand and commit to God's call to advance the Kingdom of God until everyone, and everything is under Kingdom rule. They will understand the devil's default is ungodly government, working through proud people who ignore God and the Bible.

Benchmark: Students will use their prophetic destiny and the tenor of their way to help advance the Kingdom of God everywhere they go and whatever they do.

Focus: God wants to use His people in government.

Key Scripture:

📖 For unto us a Child is born,
Unto us a Son is given;
And the government will be upon His shoulder.

And His name will be called
Wonderful, Counselor, Mighty God,
Everlasting Father, Prince of Peace.
Of the increase of *His* government and peace
There will be no end,
Upon the throne of David and over His kingdom,
To order it and establish it with judgment and
justice From that time forward, even forever.
The zeal of the LORD of hosts will perform this.
Isaiah 9:6–7.

(Reinforce this passage several different ways today. Then ask questions about what government is.)

Key Character: Joseph

Joseph—and each of his brothers—had a prophetic destiny to become a "Father" of one of the twelve tribes—or nations—of Israel. Isn't that amazing? God set Joseph apart to advance the Kingdom of God in some remarkably interesting ways.

It is important to realize God had a prophetic destiny— not only for Joseph—but for Joseph *and* each of his brothers. We will look at their names in a little bit.

But first, "Do you think Joseph and his eleven brothers had any sisters?"

The only sister listed is Dinah. That does not mean there weren't any other sisters. In the Bible, genealogies are given by the father's name and not the mother's name. Sons are listed because they carry on their father's last name. Joseph and all his brothers are listed as sons of Israel. That is why the names of mothers and daughters are seldom mentioned.

Today we will look at a chart of Israel's wives and children and then talk about them a little bit. We will number the boys in order of their birth and put them under the names of their mothers. (You can draw or take a photo and convert it to Power Point, etc.)

LEAH	BILHAH	ZILPAH	RACHEL
1 Reuben		7 Gad	11 Joseph
	5 Dan		
2 Simeon		8 Asher	12 Benjamin
	6 Naphtali		
3 Levi			
4 Judah			
9 Issachar			
10 Zebulun (Dinah)			

📖 Now these *are* the names of the children of Israel who came to Egypt; each man and his household came with Jacob: ²**Reuben, Simeon, Levi,** and

Judah; [3] **Issachar, Zebulun,** and **Benjamin;** [4] **Dan, Naphtali, Gad,** and **Asher.** Exodus 1:1–4.

How many "sons of Israel" are listed in verses 2–4? (Help them count them—11 in all). But didn't Israel have 12 sons? Can anyone name the son who was missing? (Joseph). Exodus 1:5 gives his name and tells us where he was.

📖 All those who were descendants of Jacob were seventy persons (for Joseph was in Egypt already). Exodus 1:5.

There are seasons when things seem to go from bad to worse until it is God's Kairos time or opportune time—this is when God planned it to happen. In God's perfect timing, all things work together for good.

This happened to Joseph. God set Joseph apart to rise in government to help save his family and the nation of Israel survive famine. (You may want to explain famine, using current examples.)

God used extreme measures to place Joseph in Egypt. His story shows how God can work everything for good for those who love God and are called according to His purpose (Romans 8:28).

When a parent favors one child over the rest, what do you think happens? How does this make you feel?

God had a prophetic destiny for Joseph that only God could make happen. Joseph had to keep his eyes on the Lord and continue believing even when so many bad things happened. Joseph had to keep his eyes on the Lord and trust and obey even when hurtful things happened to him.

Israel was heart-broken when his favorite wife, Rachel, died. Her sons, Joseph and his little brother Benjamin looked and acted so much like their mother. He missed their mother so much he favored her children over the children of his other wives.

Do any of you feel like some of your brothers and sisters are favored over you? How does that make you feel?

Israel's favoritism of Joseph caused problems for all his children—the one who was favored, and those who felt their dad did not love them or care very much for them. This made them mad at their dad and at Joseph!

It wasn't Joseph's fault he was treated better than his brothers. It wasn't his brother's fault they were not treated as well as Joseph and Benjamin. But when some children are treated worse than others, they must be careful not to take it personally.

Joseph's brothers were not treated badly—but they felt "less than" their brothers because they were not as loved by their father Joseph and Benjamin. It hurts when children are made to feel "less than" their siblings. They did not feel special anymore. We've all felt like this before, but God loves each one of us!

Can you imagine having one brother with the same mom and dad, ten stepbrothers, and at least one stepsister? Joseph had one father, named Jacob, whom God later renamed Israel.

It helps to remember God changed the name of Father Jacob to Israel. God wanted to make sure Israel knew his prophetic destiny was to be the father of many nations.

Still, he is called "Jacob" sometimes and Israel other times. His sons became the heads (Fathers or leaders) of the twelve tribes of Israel.

These family heads were so important, priests wore an ephod with two stones on it. Joseph's name and the name of each one of his brothers were written on these stones.

Exodus 28:9–10 says this ephod had two stones on it, each with six names on it.

The ephod was later used for making decisions. Remember, the ephod had twelve stones with a special tribal name on each one (Exodus 28:15–21).

See the illustration on the next page.

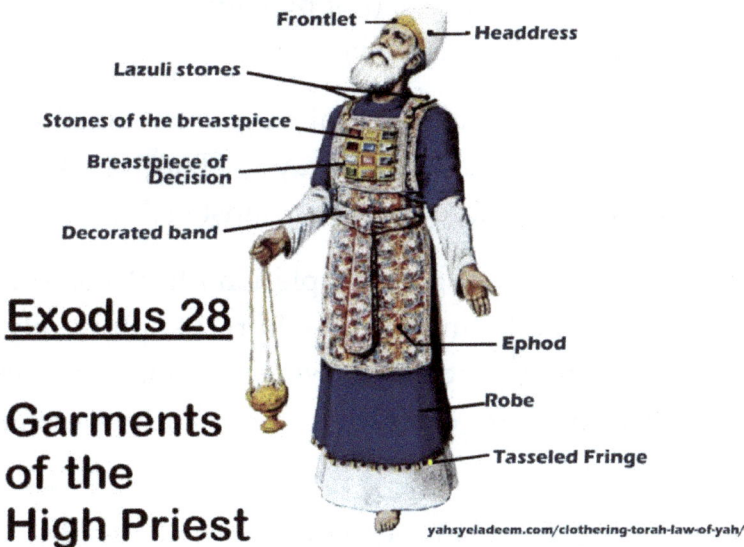

Frontlet — Headdress

Lazuli stones —

Stones of the breastpiece —

Breastpiece of Decision —

Decorated band —

Ephod

Robe

Tasseled Fringe

Exodus 28

Garments of the High Priest

yahsyeladeem.com/clothering-torah-law-of-yah/

Later, Joseph's only full brother, Benjamin, who was born of both his father Isaac and his mother Rachel was born. Sadly, Rachel died while giving birth to Benjamin.

There are times when one or both parents treat some children better than the rest. That can cause problems between parents and siblings.

Now close your eyes and let me ask some personal questions. Do any of you live with "stepbrothers or sisters?" Do some of your brothers and/or sisters have a different mom or dad than you? Do any of you feel less loved than your other "step" brothers or sisters or your "real" brothers and sisters? (Jot down their names for extra prayer and try to affirm these children in the days ahead.)

You can pray for each one (not by name) and ask any who want to talk later to let you know.

Before we stop, I want to remind you of something Jesus taught us in the Lord's Prayer. "Forgive us our sins as we forgive those who sin against us."

It is important we forgive people who hurt us. This does not mean letting people hurt us physically, emotionally, or by touching us where we don't want to be touched. In those cases, it is important to parents and/or teachers.

Forgiveness does mean choosing to forgive people for what they do and how they make you feel. Doing so gives you greater freedom and strength to do the right things.

Use any remaining time to talk about how God had a prophetic destiny for each one of these children—but how they didn't each always "know it" or "feel it" because of things that harmed them or ways they ran into difficult times in their lives.

Chapter Seven

Equipping Children to Advance the Kingdom of God

Key #7: Children must be equipped to advance the Kingdom of God. Paul's life will illustrate this.

Objective: Students will learn about and grasp God's Kingdom Mandate to advance the Kingdom of God in every level of society.

Benchmark: Students will be able to explain God's will for Christians to advance the Kingdom of God within their prophetic destiny.

Key Character: Paul

Pointer for Ministers to Children: I urge you to have a prayer list for the children and to pray for each child by name at least once a week. Your prayer list should include a listening time where you ask God for revelation as to which of the Seven Molders (Mountains) of Culture that HE wants to use them in: Family, Government/Military, Business and Commerce, Education, Religion, Media, or Arts and Entertainment.

Today we will look at the main character in the Bible who was nailed to the cross because He lived and died to advance the Kingdom of God in the whole world.

Ask: "Can you tell me who I am talking about?" (Jesus.)

Jesus is called "King of the Jews," but He really is the King of Kings and Lord of Lords (Revelation 19:16).

Jesus, however, does not rule by force. He invites people to follow Him and blesses them when they obey, but he does not force people to obey. He gives the invitation to seek first the Kingdom of God and his righteousness (Matthew 6:33).

Jesus died on the cross to advance the kingdom of God on earth. Since He rose from the dead, Jesus invites people to be born again and become part of the Kingdom of God.

Surprisingly, it was religious people and rulers who hated Jesus so much they agreed to put Him to death. When asked by Pilate if He was a King, Jesus pretty much said, "it is as you say."

Jesus died on the cross so we can receive forgiveness, but He was killed by people who did not want to be ruled by the King of Kings and Lord of Lords.

There are heroes from the Bible who have given up their lives to follow Jesus. Acts chapters six and seven tell the story of Stephen. He was one of seven men chosen to help the early apostles take care of people in need.

Stephen was full of faith and did great signs and wonders among the people. He preached Jesus but the religious leaders stoned him to death! They threw big stones and rocks at him until he died.

Thankfully, very few people must die because they follow Jesus, but there are examples in the Bible and in modern history where people are put to death because they stand for Jesus.

Later we will look at another man, Apostle Paul, who advanced the Kingdom of God on the earth. The word "Kingdom" refers to the King's Domain. Kings in the Bible ruled over specific territories like Egypt, Babylon, Medo/Persia, and Greece. The kings of these kingdoms ruled their kingdoms by force.

Many modern-day Kings still rule their Kingdoms by force. Saudi Arabia and the small island kingdom of Bahrain are both ruled by kings who rule their countries by force.

In the New Testament and today, those who choose to follow Jesus, advance the Kingdom of God.

Those who resist Jesus are used to advance the Kingdom of darkness which the devil, named Satan, rules.

Today we will begin looking at a man who, at first, fought against the Kingdom of God. Let me know when you think you know what his name is. (Saul, later named Paul.)

Saul agreed with religious people who wanted to kill Jesus and stop Christianity from spreading. But after Saul made Jesus his Lord and master, he became one of the greatest Kingdom Advancers ever.

Before looking at Paul, let's look at a man who was killed for following Jesus and then move to the one who gave his life to follow Jesus and advance the Kingdom for around twenty-five years before he was killed. Jesus said we will save our lives if we live for Him but lose our lives if we try to save them.

Key Scripture:

Then He said to *them* all, "If anyone desires to come after Me, let him deny himself, and take up his cross daily, and follow Me. ²⁴ For whoever desires to save his life will lose it, but whoever loses his life for My sake will save it.
Luke 9:23–24.

The word translated "life" in this verse can also be translated "soul."

Reinforce this verse several different ways today. Make sure they understand the connection between the Kingdom of heaven and the kingdoms of this world. Help them see their part as God answers the prayer "thy kingdom come; thy will be done on EARTH as it is in Heaven."

When Jesus taught His disciples to pray "Your Kingdom Come, You Will Be Done," He did NOT limit the Kingdom of God to church and religion.

We are supposed to pray God's will and God's Kingdom into every mountain of culture.

Jesus told us to seek first the Kingdom of God and his righteousness. Jesus wants His Kingdom people to rule the earth and everyone in it.

He wanted His Kingdom and His Kingdom people to reach out and touch everything and everyone. God wants His Kingdom to expand in every segment of society and culture, including Family, Religion, Government/Military, Business, Education, Media, and Arts and Entertainment.

Acts Chapter Seven includes a short but powerful sermon Stephen preached to a crowd of religious leaders. He quoted many verses from memory and preached such a powerful message that people either loved it or hated it. The religious leaders were cut to the heart and gnashed their teeth at him.

Stephen was so full of Holy Spirit He gazed into heaven and saw the glory of God, and Jesus standing at the right hand of God. Then he said, "Look! I see the heavens opened and the Son of Man standing at the right hand of God!" (Acts 7:54–57)

Does anyone know what happened then?

Stephen was a hero who fearlessly preached the Kingdom of God. The religious people hated him for it because he was teaching contrary to their traditions.

They dragged Stephen from the court and out of the city. People gathered around him and stoned him to death according to the law at that time.

Saul was there, but he did not participate in the stoning. He stood by to watch over the coats of those who took pleasure in stoning Stephen to his death. In other words, Saul approved of what was taking place.

God has the power to turn horrible and murderous people around to become powerful workers of the Kingdom.

Ask: Do any of you know someone who is doing wicked things and rebelling against God's will? You don't need to use their names, but what are they doing against God and His will? Let them share. You may they them pray for the people they mentioned.

What do you think God thinks of people who commit murder? Is there any hope for someone so vile?

It is amazing how wrong some religious people can be, even when they think they are doing the right thing.

Some people who think they are right with God approve of things God hates like putting unborn babies to death, approving of men marrying men and women marrying women. Some think it is good to help boys to have surgeries to become girls and for girls to have surgeries to become boys. They are right in their own eyes but wrong in God's eyes.

Saul was like that. He approved of people who killed Stephen by throwing stones at him until he died.

📖 At this they covered their ears and, yelling at the top of their voices, they all rushed at him, ⁵⁸ dragged him out of the city and began to stone him. Meanwhile, the witnesses laid their coats at the feet of a young man named Saul. Acts 7:57-58.

When we come back to Saul, whose name was later changed to "Paul," we will see how God transformed Paul and was used by God to advance the Kingdom of God in many countries and cities.

Review other Scriptures as led from Appendix A.

📖 And from the days of John the Baptist until now the kingdom of heaven suffers violence, and the violent take it by force. Matthew 11:12.

Note: Key Scriptures are listed in Appendix A, sandwiched between two verses that promise success in all we do if we meditate on the Word of God.

Appendix A

Key Scriptures to Write on Every Heart

There is one thing God says believers can do which will guarantee success in everything they do. When asked what this one thing might be, people usually suggest things like: pray, read the Bible, obey God, work hard, etc. I always tell them their answers are good but not right. The one thing guaranteeing success is meditation on the Word of God.

Children can easily memorize. We had teens in our Christian School who memorized the entire book of Philippians and were able to quote it in front of teachers in one sitting. Two students memorized the entire book of Proverbs and quoted it in entirety in one long setting.

A suggestion is for classrooms to be decorated with these scriptures, printed landscape in large typeset, and place them around the room. We begin with Psalm 1:1–3 and will end with Joshua 1:8.

Each lesson will include Key Scriptures which can be shared and expounded. It is great when a student or parent can share how each verse has played out in their own lives.

📖 Blessed *is* the man Who walks not in the counsel of the ungodly, Nor stands in the path of sinners, Nor sits in the seat of the scornful; ² But his delight *is* in the law of the Lord, And in His law he meditates day and night. ³ He shall be like a tree Planted by the rivers of water, That brings forth its fruit in its season, Whose leaf also shall not wither; And whatever he does shall prosper.
Psalm 1:1–3.

📖 Your kingdom come. Your will be done on earth as *it is* in heaven. Matthew 6:10.

📖 Now when He was asked by the Pharisees when the kingdom of God would come, He answered them and said, "The kingdom of God does not come with observation; ²¹ nor will they say, 'See here!' or 'See there!' For indeed, the kingdom of God is within you." Luke 17:20–21.

📖 Now the purpose of the commandment is love from a pure heart, *from* a good conscience, and *from* sincere faith. 1 Timothy 1:5.

📖 And now abide faith, hope, love, these three; but the greatest of these *is* love. 1 Corinthians 13:13.

📖 For I know the thoughts that I think toward you, says the Lord, thoughts of peace and not of evil, to give you a future and a hope. Jeremiah 29:11.

📖 For I know the plans I have for you," declares the Lord, "plans to prosper you and not to harm you, plans to give you hope and a future.
Jeremiah 29:11 NIV.

📖 For we are His workmanship, created in Christ Jesus for good works, which God prepared beforehand that we should walk in them. Ephesians 2:10.

📖 And whatever you do, do it heartily, as to the Lord and not to men, 24 knowing that from the Lord you will receive the reward of the inheritance; for you serve the Lord Christ. Colossians 3:23–24.

📖 For to us a child is born, to us a son is given, and the government will be on his shoulders. And he will be called Wonderful Counselor, Mighty God, Everlasting Father, Prince of Peace. 7Of the increase of his government and peace there will be no end. He will reign on David's throne and over his kingdom, establishing and upholding it with justice and righteousness from that time on and forever. The zeal of the LORD Almighty will accomplish this. Isaiah 9:6–7.

📖 From the days of John the Baptist until now, the kingdom of heaven has been forcefully advancing, and forceful men lay hold of it. Matthew 11:12.

📖 This Book of the Law shall not depart from your mouth, but you shall meditate in it day and night, that you may observe to do according to all that is written in it. For then you will make your way prosperous, and then you will have good success. Joshua 1:8.

About the Author

Douglas E. Carr was born again in 1972 and entered full-time Christian ministry in 1973. He took his first church in 1976 and worked extremely hard at the ministry. Every church he pastored grew numerically, even though he lacked the spiritual depth to lead his people from the tree of the knowledge of good and evil into the tree of life.

Doug labored hard, but with limited results, until he broke free from religious bondage and finally began letting Holy Spirit work in and through him whenever, wherever, and however he was prompted to by God.

It took a personal loss to bring Doug to where he cried out to better know God personally. After fourteen years of ministry, he was broken and left "professional" ministry for five years. For Doug, it took personal failure to help him realize just how wonderful God's love and grace really are.

Doug was restored to pastoral ministry in 1992 and has been on the quest to know and share the love, acceptance, and forgiveness of God Almighty. He has come to know Holy Spirit personally and has a great desire to lead people into freedom and victory. Now his church is not growing numerically as fast as in previous churches, but the people are becoming large in the Lord.

God has been good to Doug, blessing him with Pamela, his wonderful wife, helpmate, and partner in ministry since 12-12-93. The very meaning of the numbers in the date God chose for their wedding was indicative of how they needed to grow together in the ways of Jesus Christ and His Holy Spirit. (12 represents apostolic and/or governmental fullness)

Doug ministered his first deliverance in the mid-nineties. He soon sensed the call to lead others to freedom and began leading freedom appointments and Free Indeed Seminars.

In 1999, after a forty-day fast, Doug was led to Wagner Leadership Institute where he earned his master's and Doctorate with proficiencies in Deliverance and Intercession. While taking classes there he met Barbara Yoder and soon became part of her Breakthrough Apostolic Ministries Network.

Doug is truly blessed with His wife Pamela, and their five children, twenty-four grandchildren, and a growing number of great-grandchildren. Doug and Pam pastor His House Foursquare Church in Sturgis, Michigan, and continue to minister deep healing and deliverance, as well as lead Freed Indeed Seminars.

Their message may be heard on YouTube by date. Put: **His House Church Sturgis** in your web browser and search by date.

Dr. Carr realizes the need to raise up ministers of deep healing and deliverance who will walk in the fullness of the Spirit to bring healing and freedom to those who so desperately need it.

During the Releasing the Glory gathering at Shekinah Regional Training Center, Doug kept hearing *The Great Awakening will bring people into the churches who have tattoos and piercings everywhere you can see and many places you should never see. There will be many who have soul ties beyond numbering from recreational sex. Many have been addicted to so many substances they are now addicted to addiction. It is time for Believers to stop being afraid of the devil and his demons and stand up in faith knowing the devil and his demons are afraid of them!"*

With this word came two impressions: 1) We need to cast out the corporate spirit of the fear of the devil and demons. 2) God is waiting for the church to be ready to steward the Great Awakening so none will be lost as in the Jesus Movement. This preparation to steward the Awakening includes preparing a few from every church, or at least every city or neighborhood, to be thorough and effective in Deep Inner Healing and Deliverance.

To that end, Doug launched regional "Deliverance Ministers Equipping and Certification Programs." The seventh two-year session began on September 9, 2023.

Doug and Pam Carr also pastor His House Foursquare Church in Sturgis, Michigan where Pam's greatest call is to release the Presence of God through worship and Doug's greatest call is to equip others to do the work of the ministry in Sturgis, Michiana (Southwest Michigan and Northern Indiana region Pam and I oversee for our Apostolic Strategic Strike Force), and beyond through books and seminars.

The book you hold in your hands is Doug's thirty-first. Many of his books and other resources are available through Amazon.com, or they can be ordered directly from him.

For more information on Doug's ministry, seminars, or links to his books visit:

www.dcfreedomministry.com

Email: FreedomMinister@yahoo.com

Resources by Dr. Douglas E. Carr

Devotionals:
- *Kingdom Thoughts 101*
- *Kingdom Thoughts 201*
- *Light in the Darkness*

Deliverance:
- *Ask the Doctor about Deliverance*
- *Beat Me Up Spirits*
- *Breaking the Octopus Grip of Addiction*
- *Building on a Sure Foundation After Deliverance*
- *Busting Through to Greater Freedom*
- *Divorced! Obtaining Freedom From The Sun & Moon God by Jeanette Strauss & Doug Carr*
- *Free Indeed ~ Deliverance Ministry*
- *Free Indeed from Root Spirits*
- *From Woe is Me to WOW is He!*
- *Holy Spirit as Counselor*
- *Breaking Patterns of Perversity ~ Freedom from Iniquity*

Discipleship:
- *Choosing Kingdom*
- *Defining Moments ~ My Journey Toward the Kingdom*
- *Let's Get Real*
- *Kingdom Abundance*

Healing:
- *Kingdom Perspective: Divine Healing*

Names of God – Prayer:
- *Ancient Keys ~ Special Names*

Spiritual Gifts: Of God, Gifts, and Men (3 Vols.):
- *Ascension Gifts*
- *Motivational Charismata Gifts*
- *Holy Spirit Manifestations*

Teaching:
- *Breakthrough Essentials*
- *Getting to the Dirty Rotten Inner Core*
- *God's Say So versus Man's Know So*
- *Holidays to Shape Your Life and Transform Your Future*
- *Making Abundance a Lifestyle*
- *Schematics: God's Blueprint vs Satan's Programming*
- *Time to Act – The Enemy Snuck in While We Were Sleeping*

Free Indeed Seminars

Doug also ministers the following seminars individually or as part of an Intensive Deliverance Ministers Equipping and Certification program.

- MOD 1 Basic Building Blocks of Deliverance
- MOD 2 Deliverance from Curses, Iniquities, and the Big Five
- MOD 3 Holy Spirit Mending of Broken Hearts
- MOD 4 Free Indeed From Root Spirits
- MOD 5 From Woe is Me to Wow is He!
- MOD 6 Breaking Through to Greater Freedom
- MOD 7 Breaking the Octopus Grip of Addiction.

Doug Carr Freedom Ministries
His House Foursquare Church
410 South Clay Street
Sturgis, MI. 49091

Contact Doug
Email: FreedomMinister@yahoo.com
Web: www.DCFreedomMinistry.com

www.ingramcontent.com/pod-product-compliance
Lightning Source LLC
Chambersburg PA
CBHW060953040426
42445CB00011B/1132